# INTO THE WIND

# Into the Wind

*poems by*

Duane L. Herrmann

**OUTPOST PRESS**

AN IMPRINT OF WAYFARER BOOKS

AN IMPRINT OF WAYFARER BOOKS

Published in 2024 by Outpost Press, an imprint of Wayfarer Books
Cover Design and Interior Design by Connor L. Wolfe
Cover image © Bryce Olsen
TRADE PAPERBACK  979-8-9910415-9-1


10 9 8 7 6 5 4 3 2 1


Look for our titles in paperback, ebook, and audiobook wherever books are sold.
Wholesale offerings for retailers available through Ingram.

Wayfarer Books and Outpost Press are committed to ecological stewardship.
We greatly value the natural environment and invest in conservation.

PO Box 1601, Northampton, MA 01060

wayfarer@homeboundpublications.com

HOMEBOUNDPUBLICATIONS.COM & WAYFARERBOOKS.ORG

*"...I can hear from the whisper of the winds the sound of Thy glorification and praise..."*

—BAHÁ'U'LLÁH
*Bahá'í Sacred Scriptures*

# Contents

# INTRODUCTION

These poems are an attempt to share my positive experience with the natural world in which I was immersed while growing up on a farm in eastern Kansas: snapshots of experience. There are also, occasionally, flashes of my childhood which was not so pleasant. Those two contrasting opposites formed the person I became. One might say that some of these poems have a mystical edge— from that edge of opposites, I learned to see more than both.

The experiences related in the poems span my entire life, from just before elementary school, to my present, mature age, concluding with the words I wish to be inscribed on my stone. These provide a view of my entire life. If there are readers with challenges in their lives, I hope these poems can give them hope that those challenges need not stop them, nor prevent them from accomplishing some of their own goals.

The order of the poems roughly follows that of a seasonal year: spring through to winter.

Most Sincerely
—Duane L Herrmann

# PATH TAKEN

Path in the woods
barely trod:
do I go
and risk knowing?
What change will it make
in me, my life?
Trees whisper.
Do I listen?
Carefully—
what do they say?
Wind sings Autumn
and leaves crackle
underfoot.
What adventure is life
today?
I walk
treading lightly
with my soul.

# YOUNG GODS

They never knew I peeked.
    I was told, sternly:
"Do Not Disturb Them!"
    And I did not,
but ached to see
    those young gods,
mystical creatures:
    who wrote stories!
So, silently I crept,
    on five year legs,
toward the porch
    where I heard rain
dancing on the keys—
    music to my soul!
It was TRUE!
    They lived and breathed,
and wrote stories!
    Maybe someday I...

# LITTLE DUCKIES IN A ROW

Little farm boy
in school one day—
his new haven,
delighted to discover
he could trace
a design
through his tablet paper.
There it was!
A replica,
to the best of his ability,
of a ducky!
Now he had two!!
SUCCESS! EMPOWERED!
Three, four, five, six...
When he showed his mother
she disdained.
He continued, but
didn't show again.

# STOP IN WONDER

In a woods
in early spring
with trees bare
and grass
not evident,
shocking bright
colors:
yellow, pink, purple,
of spring blossoms
delight
eyes and soul
of one who
stumbles there,
stops
and sits to watch
them nodding
in the breeze—
while birds sing.

# SPRING HINTS

Sitting on a hillside
of barren trees
and some dead grass
waiting,
waiting for Spring,
waiting for the chorus
of spring Peepers.
It is yet too cold.
One peeped out
then retreated
to his hole secure,
home in mud.
Crows clamor and caw
but few other birds
can be heard—
wisely staying south
where it is warm.
Though air is chill,
Spring is coming
simply because
ice and snow
are finally
gone!
Seasons turn,
as seasons do,
and patience
will see us through!

# GREEN PATCHES

Little patches of green
scattered
on barren hillside
of dirt and rock and
some dry leaves.
In early Spring
this green
gives hope
that Dead Winter
has passed at last.
And these greens
will someday soon
bloom,
the earliest
in just days.
I rejoice in green
for it means
another year has come.

# WET GREEN WORLD

Freshly springtime
countryside
putting on Green
with gray skies
feeding
the green with rain.
Seasons turn
and cycle through
causing wonder
and thankfulness.
Unseen seasons
also cycle
and Spring,
in men's hearts,
is breaking.
Slowly, slowly,
Spring is breaking!

# OBSERVATIONAL

Standing on the prairie
sky all around,
the human speck
considers
the difference
between his puny form
and the vasty sky.
How can he presume
superiority, yet
scripture says
a universe is enfolded
within him,
supreme apex
of Creation.
He realizes
the "real" universe
is unseen realm
beyond this life.

# GREEN AGAIN

After a long, hard winter
to see green,
mounds and piles of green,
along the road,
in tree lines
and woods,
is delight
to eye and soul.
After barren branches
the green of life
is Sweet!
In unseen realms
growth also
is evident,
as hearts open
to embrace
all souls
of every color!

# GRASS FOREVER

Before dinosaurs,
there was grass.
Before buffalo,
there was grass.
Before humans roamed,
there was grass.
After dinosaurs,
grass remained.
After buffalo stop roaming,
some grass remained.
After humans—
will grass still remain?
The sun will shine,
there might be rain,
but will grass grow?
What will humans do
before they learn
Earth is precious?

# MATERNAL CONCERN

The room was open, clean,
empty for the first time
and freshly painted.

It was like an indoor gym.

In joy, the children ran—
running soon was tag.
Sis stood in the corner
   by the window door.
He rushed and tried to tag her.
   She jumped away.

His arm outstretched
   sliced through the glass,
   blood dripping to the elbow.

Painter yelled at him:
   "Clean up the mess!"
and checked to see
that no blood
   was on her wall.

# PRIVATE GAS CHAMBER

Didn't make,
didn't use,
as a boy when
I so desperately
needed to leave
endless work hell
that was my home.
No love there,
no affection,
just work
with no thanks
which didn't come
for decades
and only then
because I forced it.
Mother giggled,
thought I was cute.

No. Desperate!

# MORNING DREAMING

Mist rising, circling wisps
over still, smooth water.
Silence.
The morning is empty,
even the birds
have not found their voice—
waiting, waiting
for the sun
and warmth and light.
SPLASH!
Ripples cross the lake
gently rock the boat.
The boy stirs,
his sleeping nest
too warm to leave,
the dream
just within reach:
mist circling, rising...

# PRAIRIE FREE

Rolling prairie—
sheltering vales and creeks—
hilltop expanse
of sky and sky and sky
with grass blowing, waving
under wind,
constant wind.
The soul soars
into expanse
of Heaven
and one knows
humility
in the face
of vast reaches:
land and sky
spreading out
forever—
soaring!

# WHEN WATER

In the creek, running,
when water is clear:
almost, it is
invisible.
Only ripples show
substance.
Rushing over rocks
sunlight glitters,
sparkles, dances:
Water is alive!
It sings falling
over stones and tree
roots.
Rooted as am I
since some ice age
when ancestors
I cannot know
walked here.

# TRAJECTORY

Spiraling down, down, down
into darkness:
no end
no way out
no hope.

No one told me
that one day,
unavoidably,
I would be older—
old enough to leave
and NO ONE could prevent me.
I would not have to live
at home forever—
do the dragon's bidding.
I would be old enough
to LEAVE!

At seventeen,
I did.
Life became joy:
no one to care for
except myself;
no family cooking
or their laundry

or clean her house
nor screaming, screaming, screaming.

I lived
and learned love.

# SOUL SOOTHING

Boy lies in grass
in the shade
hat over face
listening
to new wind.
Trees have leaves
fresh this year
and their sound,
that soothing sound,
each new spring,
is music
to his soul.
He sleeps.
Restful, calm,
as world careens,
he is refreshed,
strengthened,
and comforted.

# WIND AND WILL

Constant Wind
blowing
1,000 miles and more
over flat land;
no mountains
in its way,
ever blowing:
a Force
not to be stopt
as the Will of God
Acts
on human lives
according to
Divine Decree,
mysterious to us,
but in the end,
beyond time,
Just.

# SKY BLUE

Sky embracing land
Sky embracing you
Sky in all directions
Sky blue
Sky free
   of clouds
Sky waiting
   for you to see
   what may be
   beyond
   next horizon.
Can you see
   what may be
   possible, practical?
   What may be
   envisioned?
Without vision
   there is no hope
   no future
   for you or me.
Below the sky
   are trees,
   creeks,
   roads,
and
   here and there:
   People!

# TREE VOICES

Leaves are back
after absence
of half a year
and trees,
once again,
have their voices.
They speak
in waves of wind:
Loudly, softly,
in a rush,
or quiet murmur.
No matter.
They speak
and my heart melts.
No longer silent
they say
what I feel
and believe!

# DEER TRACKS

In the path,
hoof prints
of deer, I know.
They use the paths
I've made
uphill and across,
yet make their own
through prairie grass
which I also walk
and glory in moonlight.
We are here
in separate times—
almost...

Suddenly we see
each other—
stare...
They flee,
and I wonder...

# PASSING BY

Shadow forms pass by
on the right, on the left,
indistinct and blurred.
What are they—
features cloaked, hidden?
Then—long stretch of nothing:
just gray on all sides,
no ground, just gray,
even straight ahead.
Alone in the cosmos—
just me, my car,
and tiny length of road.
Fog so thick,
cloud on the ground.
Some say,
this is our mind,
even on a clear day
or, spiritual perception!

# VELDT ALIVE

With wind
flowing, soaring
caught for moment
moving on
transported
without will
of its own.
Passing a tree
it's higher branches
the most nimble
flowing
with the wind
bending, swaying
floating
above the grass,
waves of grass
across the prairie
up and over the rise
down along a creek
above water rustling,
rippling over rocks
falling
down stones
swirling around
logs and boulders

and slowly flow
a ways until
lifted up as wings
above stone fence
down in places
with moss
on north side
molted
sheltering
spawning life
and new worlds.

# SEASONAL SIGHTING

Clouds arising
from the ground
rising high
into the sky
above horizon
here and there and there,
all around
billowing
high.
Not fog,
not here,
not this dry land,
and only in spring
do these clouds rise,
these clouds of smoke
from prairie fires
to clear dead grass,
enrich the soil
and keep back brush.
Ancient action,
systematic now
astonishing all
who see
and ash remains
blackened Earth
until rain
and GREEN!!

# SPRING BURNING

Meadow renewal
with burning
flames cleanse
consume
seeds unwanted
plants and sprouts
thickets, trees
crowding grass—
all gone!
Invasive species
held back,
now ash.
Grass again
can roam free
in the wind;
winter food
for livestock
and farm.

# COYOTES CALLING

Yipping in the night
of a world unknown,
unseen but heard,
parallel to human,
hidden from sight.
Their world and ours
so different!
From their view
what would be seen?

# GIVING VOICE

Those who give voice
to the voiceless
gather to share
and delight
in success when
they achieve goals
of transformation
of lives and hearts
from darkness
to understanding
and acceptance
of new visions,
new possibilities
to broaden horizons
of those with no voice
and empower them
to dream and arise
to fulfill their lives.

# LEAF WARNS ME

Leaf
hanging in air
caught, suspended
by invisible web.
Warning to my face:
there is more
that can't be seen!
I'm thankful
and avoid;
my walk
not interrupted.
Spiders have to eat,
I know,
and store food
for hatchlings,
but elsewhere—
they don't need
to block the path.

# MEADOW MINE

Meadow
on top a hill
past trees and creek
cut by fence,
almost invisible,
not dividing sky—
here can see Glory!
I go.
Take a deep breath.
Breathe
and find Peace
in shade
beneath sheltering
Trees
who carry wind
and healing
to my soul.
They speak to me:
calm,
rest,
relax,
peace,
this is true
so are you,
and in Peace
you will abide
forever!

# OPPOSITE BALANCE

A clearing in the trees
on the edge of a meadow
screened
one from the other.
A refuge
from blaze of day,
the other, open
space of vastness.
I belong to both,
need each place.
Refuge and space
are part of me—
opposites I reconcile
as we all,
spiritual-material
creatures be,
until progressing
beyond this world.

# SPIRIT SPEAKS

That small still voice
which whispers wisdom
when I'm too busy
to see.
That small still voice
has saved my life
more than once:
before mobile home fell,
before tractor flipped,
before bridge crash,
before bicycle fell
in front of my car,
before tree twisted
as it came down.

"God let you live
in hope that someday
you wouldn't be so stupid."

I can agree.

# SEASONS CYCLING

Late summer dry
leaves falling,
air is cooler—
relief
from searing heat,
soon
autumn rains
refresh the land
to begin cycling
into Spring,
just as Revelation
renews the spirit
and civilization
cycles again:
renewal, rebirth
and each time
progress
builds on.

# LAND'S SECRET

Rolling prairies
with hidden valleys
draws and gullies
holding water courses,
rivers, creeks, and streams,
and trees
sheltering life
containing wisdom
from the winds.
Secrets of the ages
speaking to those hearts
here and there
open to promptings
from the Hidden World,
realm behind
"Reality,"
but is itself
Sustaining Real.

# EAT LIKE A...

Clearing
the meadow of
all that which
I would not want
to eat  -
if I was a cow!
I'm not a cow
but,
it's not really so difficult.
I do not want
hard woody things,
or sharp pointy things,
in my mouth,
so—why would they?
And, this meadow
has plenty of both,
so the killing
is easy.

# MEADOW CLEARING

That expanse of grass
cleared now
of tiny forests:
miniature trees—
are gone.
Grass grows tall
gloriously green
an endless sea
up the horizon
deep blue sky
What do grasses say,
whispering
secrets of the sea?

Come!
Come with me!
Adventure here—
forever is
the running free!

# DANCING ON THE WIND

Wings flutter
bits of color
dancing
on the wind
I see and rejoice:
life is here,
energy and beauty
dancing
on the wind.
Sharing
from one blossom
to another,
living their lives
and stimulating
other lives—
connected
as we all are
one with another
and the planet thrives.

# PRAIRIE PICTURE

Air is clear,
rain washed,
pure blue skies.
Great white forms—
placid, silent, suspended,
still.
And below—
vast expanse of greens:
dark green trees,
vast reaches tasseling corn,
variegated lighter greens
of meadows, pastures,
and roadsides,
plus, here and there
the adornment
of a farmstead: house and barn.
Thus rolls the prairie
on midsummer's day.

# MAGICAL BUTTERFLY MOMENT

I don't know why...
I can't explain....
I didn't do...
anything unusual,
but was still.
In that stillness
came
a bit of beauty
glancing on my life,
my finger tip
and life stopt.

I was still...
hardly breathed
to prolong
magical moment
Butterfly Love
kissed my skin
rested
then flew on.

# FLY WITH ME

I want to fly
like butterflies—
with wings
colorful
bits of beauty.
Oh, that I
could also fly.
I stretch and stretch
and WINGS appear!!
Slowly dry them
in warm sun
and off
into clouds.
Finding food
I drink deep
and merge
into flower colors.
Come!
Fly with me!

# CIRCLE AND CIRCLE

A circle of space,
a circle of peace,
a circle of trees,
surrounding—
one side a valley,
the other a meadow,
I sit, listen.
Birds:
fly in, around, sing,
and pass by.
Clouds silent sail,
sun shines through
shadows on the ground,
dance with wind
flowing along.
I sit,
wait and pray,
in Mystic Streams.

# WALDEINSAMKEIT*

My sanctuary—
My refuge—
My oasis away
from the pressing crowd
and their needs.
My trees!
I go—
breathe deep
and return
to the Center:
Center
of my being.
Trees keep me
alive.
Trees tell me:
Storms will pass
and I will stand—
we stand together.

# TREES AND ME

Trees shade me
from searing sun,
and protect me
from its heat.
Branches roof my world
sheltering
from unending sky.
Leaves whisper
in the breeze
to me, saying:
Gentleness, Kindness,
is in the world—
despite
what the world
has done.
Trees breathe so we
can breathe—
species intertwined.

# WATER CYCLING

Rain won't come
it's afraid to fall,
to lose its life
in the dirt;
once there
plants will drink
and water
will be gone.
Water doesn't know
it will be released
to cycle through clouds
and live again:
just as love,
once given,
keeps on going
past all we know
and the world
keeps growing.

# MILKWEED TALE

Lone monarch feeds
on milk weed bloom—
nourishment
for long flight home.
Where?
Oh, where
are millions who
should be here too?
Decimated,
nearly extinct
by pesticides,
negligence and greed.
Superfluous, some say
ignorant of their role
in sustaining life—
not to mention
beauty
and joy.

# COMFORT RUMBLING

A gray day—finally!
Cool and damp
relieve the heat—
and long dry spell.
Clouds came at night,
slowly,
then waited
till nearly dawn.
Distant thunder rumble
means
rain is wide,
will likely stay
enough to fill
ponds and creeks and grass,
crops and livestock, so
we'll make it
through this year—
at least.

# SILHOUETTED

Lightening among the trees
flash and
flash again:
strobe illumination—
stark
against the night.
Trees witness
brightness:
stand firm.
Wind rushes passed
leaves along,
branches dance
and rain
pelts down
torrents drenching
all the world
giving life—
and air.

# BARE NIGHT ADVENTURE

In dead of night,
wee hours deep,
the man awoke
went out where
wind touched the world
and him, every inch,
all of him.
How alive he felt
and reveled in his being!
Leaves danced,
flowers nodded:
"Yes!"
He was free.
The dark kept secret—
world did not stir,
satisfied,
he returned to bed
and slept.

# SEA OF WHEAT

For those who've never seen,
from second story window,
barn loft, or tree top,
a field of wheat
nearing maturity
with heavy heads of grain
undulating under wind,
whispering.
Comparison
to ocean waves
is real.
Go some day
in June,
get above the grain,
watch the waves
crossing the field:
ocean waves
of golden grain.

# STONE FENCE

Once upon a time,
a hundred years ago,
a fence was built
of stones pickt up
from the farmer's field—
cheaper than wire,
easier than posts,
but now falling
one by one, mostly
due to winter heaving,
with north facing moss,
and holes and tunnels,
homes and safety
for tiny, little lives.
Down the hill it goes
separating meadow
from cultivation, I...
wish that fence was mine.

# LONELY LAND

Six outbuildings
one, a small barn,
no house
and just one tree;
obviously, once
there was a house
and, likely, more trees—
and flowers.
It was a family farm
but family is gone
and the farming too,
just grassland now.
Soil was too poor,
or insufficient rain,
to sustain a farming life,
or improvident decisions,
or banker's greed,
ended hopes.

# TINY STRENGTH

Walking a path
through bushes
or close trees,
a strange sensation
to feel
across bare skin—
chest or stomach:
strength,
before it breaks,
of a spider's web.

It will break
but, tension before,
and resistance,
is obvious
and amazing.
Only drawback:
if the spider
stays on you!

# PRAIRIE NIGHT WIND

Moonlight caresses
prairie waves
under wind
sweeping
north or south,
a reminder
of open space.
Clouds linger
overhead,
silent witness
in the night—
while we,
frail, ignorant,
arrogant and weak,
try and try
to direct our lives
to an end
beyond ourselves.

# MEADOW MOWED

Near decade of effort
to clear,
neglected with no access,
meadow now is all
mowed.
Miniature forest
just last year
now gone
cut and hauled away,
and rocks
that could damage
parts,
pickt up one by one;
effort now rewarded
by swaths of grass,
from end to end,
cut and drying
for cattle feed.

# SOLITARY RAKING

Grass is mowed and baled,
first time in years,
and the meadow
now looks beautiful...
Giant bales scattered
here and there
randomly it seems,
but not.
Yet,
machines can't do it
all.
Some cut-grass remains—
raking machine
could not pick up;
so I rake the clumps
to use for mulch
so dead spots
won't appear.

# PEACE PLACE

There is a clearing,
a space,
among trees
created and
obviously
separated from
the meadow.
Where is shade,
relief from sun
with some light wind.
Squirrel leaps to branch
and jays argue
over matters of Great
Importance.
Life swirls around
while I sit,
relax, appreciate
peace.

# TWILIGHT TRANSITION

Night falls
and reality
fades away.
Trees change shape
and flowers
find new forms.
Increasing darkness mends
sharp reality of blight.
I no longer need
an answer
to my name.
Butterfly teaches
lessons
for us all.
What other self
can I become?
Let's go
find out!

# TILTING... DOWN!

Shed by the side
of country road
began to lean
after owners left,
then tilt,
and continued
precariously
for decades,
while wood bees
and other littles
did their work:
making homes,
laying eggs,
and eating, eating, eating!
Then one storm,
with wind and rain,
blew through—
and it went down!

# HAND FITTING

Odd-shaped rock,
hand-size,
rounded, but broken,
found in a field
with no others or like
nearby.
The finder, late
twentieth century,
mindlessly turning,
wondering
how it came to be,
accidentally
turns it right
and use becomes clear:
human-shaped,
special,
to fit the palm of a hand
to scrape clean the skin
for curing hides
some thousands of years
before!
It was a tool
when rocks were tools
shaped for use!
How many hands,

how long ago,
had used this tool,
delight in its edge
so useful and new,
with thanks to its maker,
and what dreams
might its holder have held
of the good life
for her tribe,
her family,
and people?

# GOLDEN DAYS

The air, somehow,
has color now,
a golden tint
to echo trees
turning yellow
and ripening crops:
corn, soybeans, milo.
Cool mornings
will sometimes warm,
and the sky
is a softer blue;
all say a mellow time
to relax, yet prepare
for winter.
The year has reached
its end.

Air can't be full of dust,
can it?

# CHANGE IN AIR

Cooled autumn wind
blows over meadow
haunting grass
as it waves by.
"End is near,
soon, soon."
Not saying:
"After every end—
a new beginning."
Seasons, lives
civilizations;
even continents
and planets,
are renewed.
We must need see
far, far beyond ourselves
to the Master Plan
in operation.

# PERSPECTIVE: PATIENCE

Tree
standing
giving strength
before my life
and after,
wondering
at these forms
moving below,
sometimes killing...
I can't stop them
only moan
until hard wind,
and age and rot,
bring me down
as must I go
to nourish
new generations
of ancients.

# DRIVING SURPRISE

Dark moonless night
no road lights
two posts on the side,
two reflectors each,
driveway width apart...
But—no.
No driveway here.
Slow down!
What are...?
OH!
Dim shapes take form...
Ears!
Two deer stand still
staring at me,
as I at them.
Our lives touched
no more than this
but enough.

# I CONQUER MY WORLD

Despite dyslexia—
I read.
Despite A.D.H.D.—
I sit and write.
Despite cyclothymia—
I persevere.
Despite anxiety—
I carry on.
Despite mutism—
I speak.
Despite P.T.S.D.—
I function some.
Despite yearning
for release from life—
I live.
I don't know why,
but some times
I glimpse a reason.

# SLOW TURNING

Early autumn shadows
stretch across the land
then cool reach—
a warning of
freezing cold ahead.
Birds have fled,
except for crows
who must caw up
some notice of their own.
"Hurry! Hurry!" Do they say?
"Make way! Make way!"
Some chorus still remains
of cicada circus singing
but soon
they too will go
before the cold,
then silence
all around.

# AUTUMN DECAY

The autumn of decay
takes
exhaustion of the year
for transformation
to new hope
for next year.
Nourishment
as all things
recycle
according to plan.
Dead leaves,
bodies and bones,
all become
nutrition
for next generations,
next cycles
of life
sustaining.

# DEAD LEAVES FALL

Do they know
when they go?
Or, where?
Has all life died,
or just cold wind
carried them away?
Down
to shroud the ground,
Leaves fall
layer over layer
and, in winter,
becoming food
for other trees
and other life.
Human life turns
cycle after cycle
even
civilizations.

# SILENCING TREES

Trees become silent
as leaves fall,
cool nights, dry days
bring them down,
barren branches bend
in fierce wind,
no gentle rustling now
as tempest sweeps the Earth
no one knows
where or when,
wrecking havoc
on static institutions,
procedures
and norms
that prevent equity,
equality and unity
of our one
human family.

# BARN STANDING

Barn by itself
lonely reminder
what once was
a thriving farm,
now gone
reasons unknown,
but the barn remains
of a young man's hopes
and family dreams.

# SAVING THE FENCE

Tree with seven trunks,
all dead,
like spread fingers,
or an open fan,
against the sky,
but some falling.
More will fall
across the fence
with destruction
unless...
until...
brought down
with purpose
which was, eventually,
done.
Now, vacant space
opens the sky
with stubs remaining.

# RESPITE

Tired man sits
in his treed space
cleared
by him, for him,
from brush.
Flowers planted
and grass,
paths lined and bordered.
He brought order
and now rests,
writes too, sometimes,
of this peace,
beauty and grace
despite tumult
in his mind
tearing him,
rending him
immobile.

# DEATH JOY

Death comes with joy
at least
in my heart.
Now, I will be
FREE!!
Free of the biting.
Free of constant picking.
Free from worry of
what I wear,
yet,
it will not last,
I know,
but can ignore that now.
I am FREE
and will soon begin
my Happy Dance.
Nights are cold enough
insects have ALL DIED!

# KANSAS VELDT

With the wind
flowing, soaring
caught for moment
moving on
transported
without will
of your own.
Passing a tree
its higher branches
the most nimble
flowing
with the wind
bending, swaying
floating
above the grass,
waves of grass
across the prairie
up and over the rise
down along a creek
above water rustling,
rippling over rocks
falling
down stones
swirling around
logs and boulders

and slowly flow
a ways until
lifted up as wings
above stone fence
down in places
with moss
on north side
molted
spawning life
and new worlds.

# NOVEMBER WORLD

Gray November sky,
trees are bare again
and wind chills,
soon, I will be older.
Trees full of birds,
going one direction:
fleeing south
ahead of cold and freezing;
long waiting ahead.

# EARLY WINTER GIFT

Unseasonably warm days,
a string of them
after early blizzard:
a gift.
Autumnal snow,
a stimulus
for concentrated work
later, during warm days.
Then, with BLAST
winter hits
buries under snow
and stays,
forcing work to end
outside—
some of it, at least,
as another year
turns and we measure
accomplishments.

# WONDERING TIME

At night
wind sounds stronger,
in the dark—
more cold.
Winter time for waiting:
I wait.
No dirt can move—
frozen;
no grass grows.
What will spring bring?
How will plantlings
grow?
Each year trees
change some shape,
and earth moves under
ground.
Wait and watch.
What change will come?

# FROZEN TAN

Northern sky
of pale orange sun
filled with streaks
of pinks, blues, and whites
contrasting above
skeletons of trees,
frozen tans of grass,
fields of snow and stubble:
final colors
of a dying day.
One day and time,
one civilization,
passes for another
cycling through time
we see only
when looking far enough
across time and space
and experience.

# MID-WINTER NIGHT

Where is that "flow"?
That union where
tree reaches me?
Leaves are stripped,
wind is howling,
laced with ice.
My puny self retreats
to shelter distant
from my trees.
They are lashed
and I cower
in warmth secure.
I've abandoned trees,
they did not leave me.
Will they forgive?
Or, remember?
I can only trust
the latter will prevail.

# ADHD EXPERIENCE

A train explodes
on the stand
beside my chair—
but no one spoke,
so I could relax
until next time.
Earthquake rumbled by
the street outside
and faded eventually.
I waited for another
knowing it would come
and did—with sirens.
Squirrels thunder over
mindlessly loud
attention broken
thought derailed.
Hour after hour,
day after day after day.....

# WINTER'S GRIP

Winter's grip
will not last—
appearance is deceiving,
new life stirs
deep, deep down
at the level
of foundation.
New life,
new way of life,
for the old is dead,
and remains
appearance only:
dominating,
yet lifeless,
powerless.
New life,
new way of life—
coming!

# NO MEMORY OF NICE

She is nice now,
smiles when she sees
me,
touches me gently
with affection,
calls me:
"Sweetie," and
"My baby."
Though I'm over sixty-five,
I don't mind.
This new mother,
one I don't know,
never dreamed
would ever exist,
but had yearned...
This is strange—
I have no memory
of her nice to me.

# STRANGE YEAR

A strange year
of prolonged autumn,
midway to the equinox
it snowed
somewhat over an inch
enough
to cover the ground
and grass.
By the end next day
it had melted
except
for north facing pockets.
Spring proceeded early,
as did summer.
It would be named,
"Year of one-day winter"
if we still named years,
and more believed the warming.

# WAITING FOR SPRING

Patient, patient,
waiting for Spring!
Dead grass stalks,
barren trees,
miles and miles
of tawny prairie
in varied hues:
yellows, tans,
waiting.
But, unseen,
deep, deep down,
at basic levels
there is growth, change—
New Life;
new forms taking shape
and one day—
will sprout:
New Civilization.

# BOY'S NEWS

"Your Momma's dead,"
the man said,
stunned,
to his first grade photo.
"She can't hurt you
anymore."

Then he began
to cry.

Also died that day—
    the possibility,
    the hope,
    that someday
    she might
       love him.
In her last week
    he learned
    as she reached twice
       to hold his hand.

# SPRING IS PEEPING

New life
new growth
new social
relationships
and families
all around the globe
embracing
brown, yellow, black, red and white
coming together
in new ways
sharing new hope
for mankind
amidst
chaos and confusion
passing failure
as humanity
strives to become
one.

# DEAR MOTHER

"Mamma?"
Asks the grown deer
to the skull among
bones on the ground,
knowing this was mother.
"I've been looking
for you so long.
Why did you leave
me alone?"
Skull does not reply
there are no eyes,
jaws not attached,
even one missing.
Deer noses among them
searching for comfort
and warmth, gone
for such a long,
long time.

# WALKING WRECK

Trying to blend
with invisible wounds
no one can see,
or guess until
interactions
are noticed
as not quite right—
the result of stress
for decades
since birth.
Some days
are better than nights,
others not.
He continues to walk
trying to guess
what others
easily know as:
"normal."

# LEAF WIND

Last leaf of the day
clings tenaciously
to life and the wind,
forever the wind,
across the plains
miles and miles
to another tree,
another leaf
which also clings
in unison blowing
in the wind.
One day, I too,
will blow through
and who will see
what is left of me,
last leaf
clinging to the tree
from whence it came.

# SOUL SONGS

Soaring
in the meadow
with grass and sky,
my heart sings.
Restraints and limits
will someday pass
and I will lift beyond
imagination
to placeless place
and sing: Glory
to the One
Source of Being:
Praise.
Trivialities of life
are passed,
and Beauty
is all around,
with Joy and Joy and Joy.

# LIGHT UPON LIGHT

Beings of Light
connected by Love,
this,
true human nature.
To love and be loved
the basis
of our creation—
reason for existence.
More and more learn
this fundamental fact
of our existence.
Light reaches out
to Light and joins
even more Light
and together
radiate Love
to all existence
forevermore.

# SAY INSTEAD

When I die—
don't say,
"He died."
Instead say,
"This one day
his true love
woke him up
and
took him home!"

# NOTES

WALDEINSAMKEIT:  This title is German and roughly means: the satisfactory, contented, spiritual feeling one has when alone in the woods.  See Emerson's poem of the same title.

VELDT: another word for prairie, steppe, pampas, etc.


## Previously published credits

*Duane's Poe Tree:* Frozen Tan, Fly with Me.

*Fevers of the Mind:*  Private Gas Chamber, Trajectory

*Reiter's Block:* Saving the Fence

*Silk Road:* ADHD Experience

*Spillwords:* Kansas Veldt

*Tiny Seed Literary Journal:* Dancing on the Wind, Spring Burning.

*To the Newspapers:* Observational, Prairie Picture, Change in the Air, Hand Fitting.

*Topeka Genealogical Society Quarterly:* Barn Standing.

*Wind and Will and Other Poems:* Wind and Will, Opposite Balance, Seasons Cycling, Land's Secret, Circle and Circle, Prairie Night Wind, Twilight Transition, Dead Leaves Fall, Wet Green World, Winter's Grip, Waiting for Spring, Spring is Peeping, Light upon Light.

*Wards:* Water Cycling

# ABOUT THE AUTHOR

Duane Herrmann began making stories when he was three or four (he couldn't count, so can't remember exactly) and told stories to his younger sister soon after that. Now he tells stories to his grandchildren, they like the real ones about family history the best. As a child he was forbidden to speak, then could not learn to read (and still can't spell), but now his words, posted on the internet, have found readers all around the world.

Despite Herrmann's traumatic childhood and subsequent struggle with mental illness and emotional disabilities, he perseveres through this writing. Father, grandfather, internationally published, award-winning poet and historian, Duane Herrmann's work has been translated into several languages. He has a sci-fi novel, eight full-length collections of poetry, and several chapbooks. His poetry has received the Robert Hayden Poetry Fellowship, inclusion in American Poets of the 1990s, Map of Kansas Literature, Kansas Poets Trail, 2023—Keweenaw Interactive Art Walk, and others. His historical offering, *By Thy Strengthening Grace*, received the Ferguson Kansas History Book Award. He holds degrees in education and history.

# OUTPOST
## PRESS

AN IMPRINT OF WAYFARER BOOKS

At Wayfarer Books we believe poetry is the language of the earth. We believe words—shaped like rivers through wild places—can change the shape of the world. We publish poets and writers and renegades who stand outside of mainstream culture—poets, essayists, and storytellers whose work might withstand the scrutiny of crows and coyotes, those who are cryptic and floral, the crepuscular, and the queer-at-heart. We are more than just a publisher but a community of writers. Our mission is to produce books that can serve as a compass and map to all wayfarers through wild terrain.

## WAYFARERBOOKS.ORG

# WAYFARER

BASED IN THE BERKSHIRE MOUNTAINS, MASS.

At Wayfarer Books we believe poetry is the language of the earth. We believe words—shaped like rivers through wild places—can change the shape of the world. We publish poets and writers and renegades who stand outside of mainstream culture—poets, essayists, and storytellers whose work might withstand the scrutiny of crows and coyotes, those who are cryptic and floral, the crepuscular, and the queer-at-heart. We are more than just a publisher but a community of writers. Our mission is to produce books that can serve as a compass and map to all wayfarers through wild terrain.

WAYFARERBOOKS.ORG

www.ingramcontent.com/pod-product-compliance
Lightning Source LLC
Chambersburg PA
CBHW020413130626
46549CB00006B/2545